Cloud Security For Dummies®

A Wiley Brand

Netskope Special Edition

by Lebin Cheng, Ravi Ithal,
Krishna Narayanaswamy,
and Steve Malmskog

For Dummies®
A Wiley Brand

Cloud Security For Dummies®, Netskope Special Edition

Published by
John Wiley & Sons, Inc.
111 River St.
Hoboken, NJ 07030-5774
www.wiley.com

ISBN 978-1-119-06304-9 (pbk); ISBN 978-1-119-06303-2 (ebk)

Manufactured in the United States of America

10 9 8 7 6 5 4

For general information on our other products and services, or how to create a custom *For Dummies* book for your business or organization, please contact our Business Development Department in the U.S. at 877-409-4177, contact info@dummies.biz, or visit www.wiley.com/go/custompub. For information about licensing the *For Dummies* brand for products or services, contact BrandedRights&Licenses@Wiley.com.

Publisher's Acknowledgments

Some of the people who helped bring this book to market include the following:

Writer: Rebecca Senninger

Development Editor: Elizabeth Kuball

Project Editor: Elizabeth Kuball

Acquisitions Editor: Amy Fandrei

Editorial Manager: Rev Mengle

Business Development Representative: Karen Hattan

Project Coordinator: Melissa Cossell

Table of Contents

Introduction

Employees expect to work efficiently and flexibly wherever they are — at the office, at home, or on the road — using the most convenient way possible — whether that's with a desktop computer, laptop, tablet, or smartphone.

Increasingly that means people are getting their jobs done using cloud services. It also means that sensitive company data is being uploaded, downloaded, and shared on a daily basis.

And many times, the apps being used to do that work aren't being used safely. That's where *Cloud Security For Dummies,* Netskope Special Edition, comes in.

About This Book

You may be intimidated by the idea of doing business in the cloud. But chances are, even if you don't know it, you probably are. Today, people buy and deploy cloud services often without IT's permission or involvement. This is called "shadow IT." The question it brings up is: How do you keep your information secure when it's out of your control? This book helps you get started on your journey! Here you find the information you need to confidently adopt the cloud:

- Discover the cloud apps that employees are already using in your enterprise.
- Understand how employees are using these apps.
- Assess each app's risk level.
- Adopt a cloud policy tailored to fit the way you do business.
- Monitor ongoing cloud app usage and enforce compliance.

By applying the principles outlined in this book, you can make a successful transition from using traditional on-premises applications to cloud-based applications.

Icons Used in This Book

Throughout this book, you find special icons to call attention to important information. Here's what you can expect:

The Tip icon marks tips and shortcuts that you can take to make a specific task easier.

The Remember icon marks the information that's especially important to know.

The Technical Stuff icon marks information of a highly technical nature that you can safely skip over without harm.

The Warning icon tells you to watch out! It marks important information that may save you headaches.

Beyond the Book

If you find yourself wanting more information after reading this book, go to `www.netskope.com`, where you can get more information about Netskope's products. You can find webinars, reports on the state of the cloud, best practices videos, and much more!

Where to Go from Here

If you're new to the cloud, start with Chapter 1 to check out not only why cloud adoption is essential for business success, but also why doing it securely is critical. Otherwise, check out the table of contents to find a topic that interests you!

Chapter 1

Assessing the Current State of Cloud Security

In This Chapter

- Taking a look at the cloud adoption trend in business
- Assessing the use of sanctioned and unsanctioned apps
- Employing a cloud access security broker (CASB)
- Using apps securely on mobile devices and ecosystems

The number of cloud apps being used in the enterprise is growing daily. This should come as no surprise: Cloud apps are easy for users to buy and require minimal effort to get up and running. Not only are cloud app adoption rates high, but users find that they can get their jobs done more quickly and flexibly with them. Furthermore, cloud apps often lend themselves well to mobile access, so growth in mobile has only served to increase their usage.

Social media apps (such as Twitter and LinkedIn) and file-sharing apps (such as Google Drive, Box, and Dropbox) are the most visible apps. But companies are also adopting the cloud for other purposes, whether for human resources (HR), finance, customer relationship management (CRM), or business intelligence.

In this chapter, you find out why you should integrate the cloud into your daily business, the platforms you can use, and how to address any security concerns as you make the transition from a business that runs on traditional software to one that runs on cloud services.

Cloud is no longer a question — it's the way business is done.

Understanding the Growth of Cloud Adoption

When you think about cloud app growth in business, you probably think it's mostly people accessing file-sharing apps like Box and Dropbox. However, enterprise cloud adoption goes beyond file sharing. Entire functional groups — including marketing, human resources, finance, and software development — are doing business in the cloud.

Reasons for cloud adoption

Put simply, the cloud allows employees to get their jobs done more quickly, easily, and flexibly than traditional computing tools. Here are some reasons any organization — including yours — should consider embracing the cloud:

- **Business agility:** People want to be productive now; they don't want to wait until the next software rollout happens. Many cloud apps have more frequent release schedules than traditional software, which allows your company to take advantage of the latest feature sets.
- **Device choice:** The cloud gives people the flexibility to work on whatever device they want — a desktop, laptop, tablet, or phone — whenever they want. Turn to the upcoming section "Accessing the Cloud Securely from a Mobile Device" for more information.
- **Collaboration:** The cloud allows colleagues and business partners to share and access data in a seamless, frictionless way.
- **Minimal expense:** Deploying, maintaining, and updating on-premises software (along with the infrastructure to run them) can be expensive. You can reduce the expense of doing business, as well as more closely match expense with value, by using cloud apps.

Because the reasons for cloud adoption are so compelling, your employees are most likely already using cloud apps without your knowledge (see "Checking Out Cloud App

Security and Shadow IT," later in this chapter), which can put your business at risk of data compromise or noncompliance. Officially adopting cloud apps allows you to set norms and establish policies to keep your sensitive corporate data secure and maintain compliance with regulatory policies.

Types of cloud offerings

When you're ready to start doing business in the cloud, you can choose one or more of the following. While all three are being adopted at a rapid clip, this book is focused mostly on SaaS because it is the most fragmented of the types, with thousands of choices across dozens of business categories.

- **Infrastructure as a service (IaaS):** This is the most basic model of cloud service. With this model, you outsource equipment for your day-to-day business operations, including storage, hardware, servers, and networking components. The service provider owns, houses, runs, and maintains the equipment. An IaaS gives you the most flexibility for your applications, but it requires operations expertise and development resources.
- **Platform as a service (PaaS):** With PaaS, you build your applications on top of a platform with a well-defined software development kit (SDK). The application is deployed on the PaaS vendor's datacenters. With PaaS, you have fewer items to set up and don't need as many development resources as IaaS, but you're still responsible for development and monitoring.
- **Software as a service (SaaS):** With SaaS, you use apps over a network — typically, the Internet — that the vendor makes available for your use. SaaS gets you up and running quickly because it works right out of the box and you don't need any additional development resources. On the downside, you're completely dependent on the vendor for additional features.

REMEMBER

No matter which model you choose (and you may end up with more than one), your corporate data is stored in the cloud, so you run the risk of unauthorized users accessing your data. If you use the cloud, consider establishing fine-grained cloud data loss prevention (DLP) policies to help you manage what gets stored in the cloud, how it gets stored, and what stays on-premises.

Checking Out Cloud App Security and Shadow IT

Apps or systems that are deployed and maintained by people or departments outside of IT's knowledge are known as *shadow IT.* If you assess cloud apps in your organization, you'll likely find that employees use both *sanctioned* and *unsanctioned* apps:

- **Sanctioned cloud apps:** Apps that the company provides for employee use and of which IT is aware. IT usually has full administrative control over these cloud apps and maintains them on behalf of the business.

  REMEMBER: Even though IT may manage sanctioned apps, the department still may lack specific knowledge about how users are accessing these apps and what activities they're performing, including uploading, downloading, sharing, or editing corporate data.

- **Unsanctioned cloud apps:** Apps that the company doesn't know about. Very often, if IT doesn't provide the necessary tools to accomplish a needed business function, employees go outside of IT and procure their own apps. Employees can easily find, pay for, download, and administer these apps without IT's knowledge or assistance.

  On the one hand, this is a good thing because it gives employees a way to work efficiently. On the other hand, these unsanctioned cloud apps create risk for IT. Keeping apps — and the data within them — secure is impossible when IT doesn't know about them. IT can't properly enforce security or compliance in unsanctioned apps. Without important security features, such as strong user authentication and audit logging, these apps, and the data within them, are vulnerable to inadvertent or intentional data exposure.

  Finally, IT has no idea how users are using unsanctioned apps. Are they uploading sensitive data to high-risk apps, sharing data outside the company, or downloading to a mobile device?

TIP: Safely enabling the cloud means you not only manage all the sanctioned apps but also find the unsanctioned cloud apps in use. You can then begin securing the apps and data, including implementing strong authentication, monitoring administrator and user activities, and preventing data leaks. IT can consistently manage and secure all the cloud apps running across the company and enforce security and compliance controls.

Addressing Cloud App Security: CASB Solutions

IT departments have limited visibility when it comes to apps in the cloud — especially with shadow IT. They have no efficient way to track app usage or control sensitive data after it's uploaded. To bridge the gap in security, you can deploy a CASB.

The advantage of a CASB is that it allows an organization to use the cloud without compromising compliance or security. By combining security functions within a single enforcement point, CASBs also reduce the complexity of securing data in the cloud.

Some key capabilities CASBs enable include

- **Discover and assign a risk score to all apps.** They discover and assign a risk score to each identified app. This allows you to decide whether apps are acceptable for business use.
- **Provide identity-based access management.** They enable you to tap into your directory services and secure user access to cloud apps. They allow you to easily provision and deprovision user access.
- **Monitor and set up alerts for users and admins.** They help you understand user activity and its context (for example, who's sharing content outside the company). They may also alert you to anomalous activities or activities that could lead to data loss or exposure. Figure 1-1 shows a report that gives you insight into which activities were deemed risky and which were not.

- **Prevent cloud data leakage.** They enable you to enforce policies that prevent leakage of your sensitive company data from cloud apps.
- **Coach users.** They enable you to coach users about risky apps and guide them to less risky alternatives, as well as provide feedback to users about noncompliant activities.
- **Monitor for malware.** They should monitor for the presence of malware or anomalies that could indicate malware activity within cloud apps.

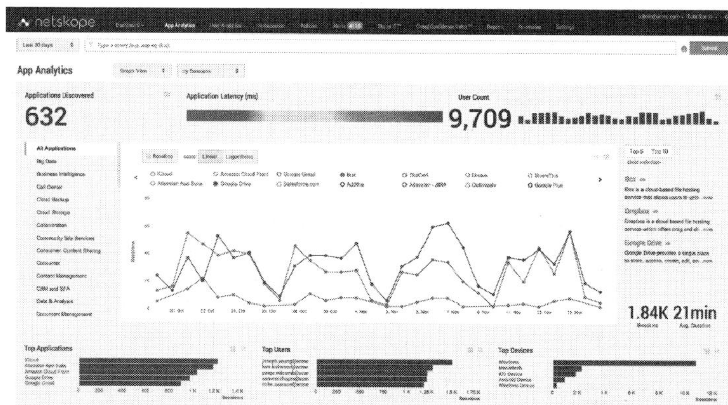

Figure 1-1: You have an easy way of monitoring app use.

REMEMBER

If your employees use their personal devices to access company information in the cloud, there's no need to discontinue the practice. A CASB can keep your business data secure while still giving your employees the flexibility to get their jobs done.

Accessing the Cloud Securely from a Mobile Device

It's hard to find a business user today who doesn't use one or more mobile devices to get work done. Users want to be agnostic in how they access cloud apps, and they often do so from multiple types of devices over the course of a single day.

You probably already give employees a variety of choices for how they can access cloud apps. These choices are a good thing, but they can also increase the risk to your sensitive business data. More than a third of all cloud data leakage policy violations occur on mobile devices.

Employees may not even be aware of your organization's mobile and cloud policies. After adopting cloud apps and enabling mobile access to them, you need to make sure users understand what the policies are, how to follow them, and the consequences of noncompliance.

Accessing Apps through an Ecosystem

Many popular cloud app vendors encourage ecosystems, or third-party apps that integrate with them to share data and enable solutions that one app by itself may not be able to achieve. Anchor tenant apps typically do this by providing application programming interfaces (APIs) to their ecosystem partners. By using those APIs, those partners can share data back and forth with the anchor tenant app.

For example, the enterprise file-sharing and collaboration app, Box, has an ecosystem of more than a thousand app partners that access and share content with Box to facilitate extended use cases such as electronic signature workflows, business intelligence reporting, and project management.

It's important to note that, while an anchor tenant app like Box may have security features built in, its ecosystem apps may not be as enterprise-ready. Because those apps may share your content, you need to have similar visibility and control across not just the main app but the ecosystem as well.

Chapter 2

Finding and Evaluating Cloud Apps in Your Enterprise

In This Chapter

- Finding the apps in your enterprise
- Evaluating the risk of those apps
- Deciding whether to block apps

Cloud apps help your people get their jobs done more efficiently. But they're hardly risk-free. How can you ensure an app is in line with your organization's policies? Offers the right level of data encryption? Has a disaster recovery plan in place? In short, how do you know if an app is enterprise-ready?

Organizations have an average of 579 cloud apps in use. Of these, 88.7 percent are *not* enterprise-ready, meaning they fail to meet enterprise standards for security, auditability, and business continuity. In this chapter, you learn the process you go through to find your apps, evaluate their enterprise-readiness, and assess whether you should block their use in your environment.

Discovering Cloud Apps: Perception versus Reality

You're ready to adopt a cloud app policy. The first step, of course, is finding all the apps currently in use in your company. You may think that most apps fit right in with company policy, but the reality is that most apps that people use — even apps sanctioned by IT — are not enterprise-ready.

TIP

To get a complete picture, look for apps accessed from desktops and laptops within the office, as well as from home computers and mobile devices, regardless of whether the apps are web-based or native, such as a sync client.

Table 2-1 shows the number of apps that people typically use in the enterprise, along with the percentage of apps that are not enterprise-ready in terms of security, auditability, and business continuity.

In addition to the consumer and prosumer apps that you expect to find in use — such as Twitter, Dropbox, and Evernote — line-of-business apps are actually the most prevalent. The marketing category has the most apps, followed by collaboration, human resources (HR), productivity, and storage.

Later in this chapter, you can find out how to evaluate the risk these apps pose, as well as whether you should block them from being used.

Table 2-1 Apps Per Category Not Enterprise Ready

Category	*Number per Enterprise*	*Percent That Aren't Enterprise Ready*
Marketing	60	98%
Collaboration	38	84%
Human resources	36	96%
Cloud storage	31	77%
Productivity	31	90%
Finance/accounting	29	98%
Customer relationship management (CRM)/sales force automation (SFA)	24	91%
Software development	23	90%
Social	16	71%
Project and program management	15	69%

Report findings are based on tens of billions of cloud app events seen across millions of users and represent usage trends from July 2014 through September 2014.

TIP: Don't underestimate the number of unsanctioned apps being used in your company. Many companies underestimate that number by about 90 percent.

Evaluating the Risk of Cloud Apps

Companies that embrace the cloud must first understand, manage, and minimize the inherent risks in each cloud model.

You can evaluate the enterprise readiness of an app based on objective criteria in the following functional areas:

- Identity and access control
- File sharing
- Data classification
- Encryption
- Audit and alert
- Certifications and compliance
- Disaster recovery and business continuity
- Security vulnerabilities and exploits
- Capability to proxy traffic for inspection and security controls

Evaluate apps based on these objective measures, covered in the following sections.

Inherent risk

When your sensitive business data resides outside of your company, you take on a level of *inherent risk*. You're storing data and — depending on the functionality from the public cloud — losing your capability to have physical access to the servers hosting your information. As a result, potentially business-sensitive and confidential data is at risk because of the inherent capabilities of the apps in which they reside. For example, if the app doesn't separate one tenant's data from another's or doesn't offer access controls as part of its service, your data is beholden to those deficiencies. As a buyer, implementer, or approver of such services, you need to ensure that the inherent security capabilities you require are available in the cloud apps your organization is using. It is important to ensure that security measures, such as securing data at rest, are in place whenever data is stored in the cloud, because this is no longer in your control and you're dependent on the security of the cloud service providers.

TIP

Your apps should follow these practices in order to limit your inherent risk:

- **Certifications and compliance:** Your apps and the datacenters in which they're hosted should be in compliance with regulations and industry guidance that matter to your business. The nearby sidebar explains the key certifications you should consider.
- **Data classification:** Apps that deal with your corporate data should enable you to classify that data according to your requirements. Those classifications can include public, confidential, and sensitive. Classifying your data enables you to
    - Define which data can be stored in cloud apps and which must remain on-premises.
    - Enforce policies on different types of data, including access and data protection policies.
    - Automatically expire access to sensitive data via policy.

  REMEMBER

  Related to data classification is data ownership. Be aware that some apps specify who owns data (the vendor or the customer) that resides in an app as part of the terms and conditions. For any apps that contain your business-critical data, only choose apps that specify that *you* own the data. Also look for terms that specify the process for retrieving your data should you discontinue the service.
- **Disaster recovery and business continuity:** Your apps should provide very clear details about disaster recovery plans and processes. Those details should reflect your business requirements for uptime and data access depending on criticality of the data. Know where your backup off-site location is, what the provider's disaster recovery plan is, and how your data will be backed up and failed over.
- **Encryption:** Your apps that store sensitive or regulated data should offer encryption of data at rest and should

give you choices for how to manage those encryption keys per your policies. (Find out more about encryption in Chapter 4.) Moreover, they should ensure that your data is managed separately from other tenants in the same cloud.

- **Capability to proxy traffic:** Your apps should enable you to inspect traffic to perform analytics and enforce your policies in real-time.
- **Audits and alerts:** Your apps that deal with critical business processes, contain sensitive data, or have access to your enterprise systems should offer robust administrator, user, and data access logging and alerting features (see Figure 2-1). This helps you detect noncompliant behavior as it's happening, as well as perform forensic audit trails after a suspected event occurs.

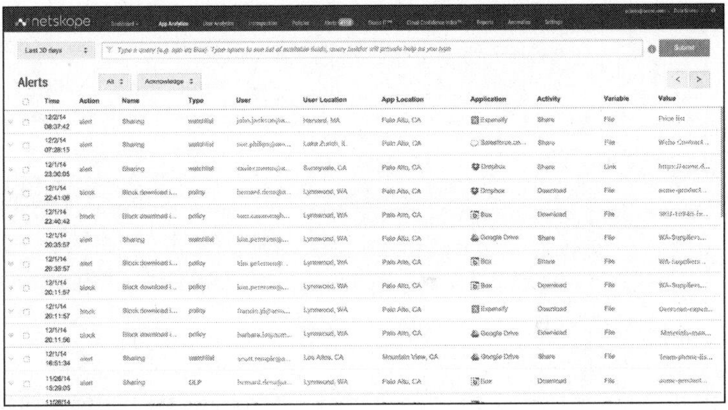

Figure 2-1: A real-time alert.

- **Policy enforcement and access control:** Your apps should offer access controls and policy enforcement commensurate with your on-premises controls. These include features such as multifactor authentication, single sign-on support, and granular access controls.
- **File sharing:** Your apps that deal with your files should support file capacities that meet your large-file requirements. This will ensure that people will use the corporate cloud apps available to them and will be less likely to seek out a potential lower-quality app — and one that you have no visibility into — to support their file sharing requirements.

Common cloud security certifications

When it comes to certifications regarding apps, the cloud, and cloud security, you should be familiar with a few key certifications:

- **SOC-1, SOC-2, and/or SOC-3:** With these certifications, you get a baseline for physical and logical access, data security, and business continuity procedures of your data wherever it's housed. Make note of whether the certification is Type I or II; the former reports on the existence of control procedures, while the latter verifies those procedures in practice.
- **SAS-70/SSAE-16:** This certification details how you report on compliance controls, and how your system matches your control objectives.
- **ISO27001:** This certification defines a top-down approach for information security management. It includes a six-part process, including policy definition, scope, risk assessment, risk management, control objectives, and statement of applicability.
- **The latest HIPAA regulation:** This regulation ensures privacy of personal health data, if applicable.
- **The latest PCI-DSS security standard:** This security standard ensures privacy of personal credit card information, if applicable.
- **Safe Harbor certified:** With this certification, users are informed if the app gathers their personal information and what that information will and won't be used for.
- **TRUSTe certified:** This certification indicates that the app has undergone a privacy assessment and audit for data privacy and regulatory requirement adherence.

Contextual risk

Before you even begin inspecting content and enforcing policies to protect data, you need the relevant context of the activity.

Your CASB should allow you to see the following details:

- Which users and user groups are using specific apps
- What apps they're using
- What devices and browsers they're on

- Where they're located
- Activity details (whether they're uploading, downloading, sharing, or viewing data)
- Which users are sharing, what they're sharing and with whom, and whether recipients are outside the company

In the next section, you find out why these details are important. Not all activities are harmless!

Cloud app activities: Not all are created equal

It's not enough to know what apps are running in your organization; you also need to understand what activities people are using those apps for.

Your cloud vendor should give you granular-level detail to all app activities, and provide you with real-time alerts when an action violates policy. (See the earlier section on inherent risk for more on alert functionality.)

Downloading, uploading, sharing, or simply viewing data are all activities that can be benign for one employee, and not so benign for another:

- A professional in the human resources department who is working at the headquarters office may have a legitimate reason to download salary information from a cloud-based HR app to perform analysis. However, a similar professional working in a satellite office probably has no business downloading the same salary information.
- An authorized employee in the finance department may need to edit field-level data within a cloud-based financial management app. However, a different, unauthorized employee in the same finance department may need only to view documents, but not actually edit any of them.
- A business development professional may have a legitimate reason to share a presentation with a partner from a file-sharing app. However, it may not be wise to allow professionals from investor relations to share spreadsheets outside of the company from the same app during the company's quiet period.

These are all situations you'll want to know about right away to prevent potential data exposure or noncompliant activity.

Here are activities you need to make sure are secure:

- **Activities that can get you into trouble:** Cloud app activities that create the most policy violations on average include login, view, download, edit, upload, and create.
- **Activities on mobile devices:** Half of all cloud app activities occur on mobile devices, with more than half of send, approve, and download activities occurring on mobile. It's important to consider risks that are unique to mobile devices when you're setting policies in your cloud apps.

With contextual information in hand — such as who the users or groups are, what app or app category they're in, what device they're on, and what activity they're performing — you can be precise in identifying potential risky scenarios so you can protect your organization and its data in a targeted way. This helps you increase the accuracy of sensitive data detection and protection.

Cracking Down: To Block or Not to Block?

As you find unknown apps, you'll probably be inclined to simply block them if they pose a risk. After all, up until now the only choices you've had have been *allow* or *block.*

Blocking policies don't work as well these days because people can usually get around your "no." They may seek an exception, go off-network and connect directly to a cloud app, or use a mobile app. Because many of the cloud apps in question are actually used for legitimate business purposes that make the company more productive and competitive, exceptions need to be made. In fact, the majority of app activity happens in apps for which IT has made exceptions. This phenomenon is called *exception sprawl.*

But with cloud apps you *can* take a more nuanced approach to deciding whether to block or not. Instead of taking a simple binary approach to the apps people want to use, you could say "yes" to nearly all their apps. Then, like a surgeon, you could slice out certain activities to make the usage of those apps acceptable to your company from a security and compliance standpoint.

This approach would put you in the position of partnering with and enabling the business rather than saying "no" in a wholesale way. And for the cloud apps that the company is slow to adopt because of security and compliance concerns, this approach lets you adopt them more quickly.

Taking a scalpel instead of a sledgehammer to the problem paves the way to cloud confidence.

The tool you use to manage your apps should let you create sophisticated, precise policies quickly and enforce those policies in real-time.

In Chapter 4, you find out why enforcing policies on activities and data, rather than blocking apps outright, is often the right choice for businesses today.

Chapter 3

Putting Cloud Security in Practice

In This Chapter

- Understanding how the apps in your environment are being used
- Logging activities
- Finding anomalies

Cloud apps are an increasing part of doing business today, with thousands of apps being using across virtually every function. But many times, those apps are not being used safely or in accordance with company policy — if there is a policy.

As you make decisions and institute policies to make those apps secure and compliant, you're becoming cloud confident.

In this chapter, you take the steps you need to be cloud confident. (In the next chapter, you learn how to create a policy for employees to follow.)

Discovering Cloud Apps

The first step is always to know exactly which apps people are using in your organization. Your CASB should give you a snapshot of all the enterprise-sanctioned cloud apps as well as discover any unknown apps in use.

After those apps are discovered, IT should evaluate each of the discovered apps against a set of objective criteria:

- Score apps on enterprise-readiness, as measured by security, auditability, and business continuity.
- Evaluate those apps' risk based on your organization's usage of them.
- Make risk-based decisions about whether to standardize on, and migrate users to, certain apps.

Evaluating app use

After you know what cloud apps everyone in your company is using, you should be able to drill down into the information surrounding those apps and understand how people are using them.

This step actually involves understanding the contextual usage of those apps:

- **Drill down into user identity.** This includes
  - An individual or group defined in your enterprises directory
  - Where people are when they access the apps
  - What devices and browsers they are using
- **Understand the app.** This includes the apps or *app instances* (different tenant accounts created within an app) that are being accessed and by whom.
- **Ascertain cloud app activities.** This includes
  - What app services users are consuming
  - What discrete actions they're taking (for example, log in, modify data, download content, upload content, share content, and administrative activities like escalation of privileges)
- **See content details.** This includes
  - What content type and file or object name they are dealing with
  - Whether the content is deemed sensitive given your organization's data loss prevention (DLP) profiles
  - Where and with whom data is being shared

  - User location
  - App location

- **Discover sensitive content.** You're looking for the content existing at rest within an app, including any that violate a DLP profile. Figure 3-1 shows you the exposure of your sensitive data in your sanctioned cloud apps.

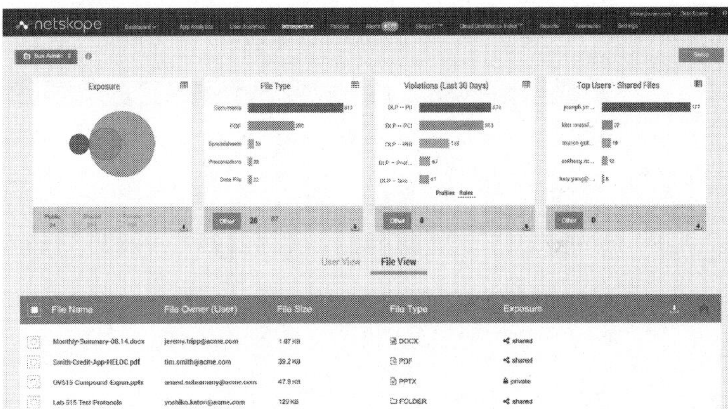

Figure 3-1: Understand exposure of sensitive content in cloud apps.

You also get one consistent view across app behaviors and can use that view to enforce one simple policy uniformly across all relevant apps instead of having to set policies app by app. For instance, *share* and *send, download* and *save,* and *edit* and *change* can each mean the same thing across different apps.

With a cloud policy in place, you don't have to analyze app after app. All the user activities should be normalized across each category of apps so you don't have to understand each app and map its activities to understand what's going on.

Auditing Activities

The capability to audit activities is critical to show accurate forensic audit trails of who has accessed each app and what he or she did.

To audit activities, you need to understand user activity and its context. For example, who's downloading from HR apps or who's sharing content outside the company?

A CASB should let you query your security data and answer any business or security question, understanding the *who, what, when, where,* and *with whom* of any user's or administrator's activity within a cloud app, users' activity overall, or activity compared to a baseline. You can

- Perform granular queries.
- Be alerted to granular behavioral anomalies; see Figure 3-2 for a report on anomalies.

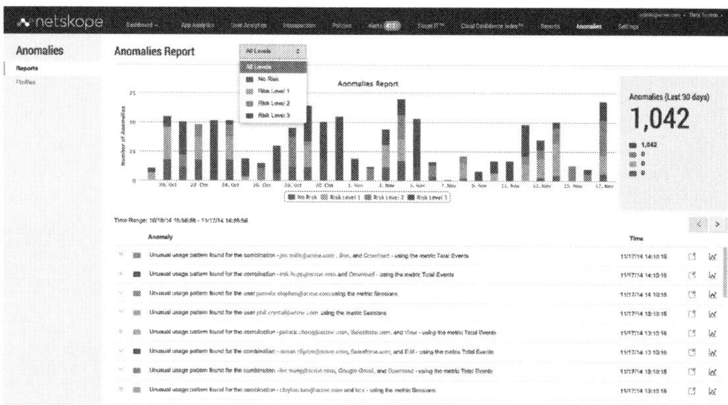

Figure 3-2: Find all the anomalies that violate cloud policy.

- Do forensic analysis after a security incident or breach.
- Set watch lists that alert you on any activity.
- Run analytics on app performance, slicing by any of the visibility parameters.
- Run deep analytics on user behavior, pivoting around parameters.
- View user behavior and activity against baselines to uncover anomalies.
- Analyze cloud app performance, uptime, latency, and service-level agreement (SLA) adherence.
- Perform forensic analysis on user activity leading up to an incident or breach.

You must be able to analyze any activity against policy, pivoting around any of the parameters. You must also be able to use analytics to detect anomalies to identify risky behavior and potential data loss or breach.

Depending on your business operations and regulations, compliance-oriented questions will rise to the top. IT should be able to answer specific questions. Here are a few examples:

- "Who from my call center in Bulgaria is accessing my CRM system, and what specifically is he or she doing?"
- "Who from my Investor Relations group is sharing docs from our cloud storage app during the company's 'quiet period'?"
- "Has any non-HR manager downloaded salary data in any cloud app in the past three months?"
- "Is there any excessive downloading or sharing that could signal a data breach?"

TIP

When you set a policy once, you can set it to be carried out across all the apps you want it to. So, when you set a granular policy such as "Let people in my call center use CRM, but don't let them download customer contacts onto a mobile device if they're outside my country," or set policies about what apps you will and won't allow based on their risk score, you know that those policies will be enforced immediately before an undesired act occurs, and you can do it at network speed across the entire business.

Beyond viewing app access and activity at a certain point, you should also have the capability to do *continuous compliance* — ongoing and uninterrupted visibility of all activities that could impact compliance with your organization's policies. IT should be able to turn any analytics query into a watch list or report, where any defined event or any deviation from a baseline will trigger an action. For example, you can set up watch lists to do the following:

- **Uncover suspicious behavior, prove a breach occurred, and clearly demonstrate malicious or even criminal activity.** You can create a granular cloud activity audit trail following a suspected event, such as the theft of sensitive content upon employee departure. For example, an employee logged into Microsoft SharePoint or OneDrive using corporate credentials, downloaded sensitive content, logged into a totally different app such as Dropbox or Google Drive using personal credentials, uploaded that same content, and then shared it with a new employer. IT should be able to construct a forensic audit trail showing every cloud app action for that user leading up to and immediately following the incident.

- **Reconstruct activities to understand just what that user did with which content in which app, and if he shared the content, with whom he shared it.** You can create a granular cloud activity audit trail following a suspected event such as the theft of sensitive content upon employee departure. For example, an employee logged into Microsoft SharePoint or OneDrive using corporate credentials, downloaded sensitive content, logged into a totally different app such as Dropbox or Google Drive using personal credentials, uploaded that same content, and then shared it with a new employer.

Detecting Anomalies

You also need to be able to detect anomalies. For example, find out when an employee is excessively downloading, sharing, or uploading data from an app, or logins from multiple locations. These usage anomalies can indicate compromised credentials, out-of-compliance behaviors, and even the presence of malware.

WARNING!

If an app doesn't support multifactor authentication, several anomalous attempted logins may be an indicator that someone is trying to hijack the user's account. Your CASB should offer protection by alerting you to the attempted access, preventing further access to the app, and reporting on any attempted accesses for security and compliance purposes.

TECHNICAL STUFF

Behind the Netskope scenes

So, how exactly does Netskope gain visibility and enforce policy dynamically on your enterprise's cloud app transactions and traffic? It enables and has production deployments on non-mutually exclusive, in-line, and out-of-band deployment options. Each of these methods has a different level of theoretical coverage, visibility, and enforcement, from the most basic to the most advanced and real-time, so it's important to choose the right one(s) to facilitate your use cases.

Out-of-band options are

- **Log-based discovery:** You can upload logs from your perimeter networking equipment such as your web gateway or next-generation firewall to Netskope offline. Log analysis provides you information about what apps you have, and the Netskope Active Platform categorizes them, gives you a view of their enterprise-readiness, and gives you a risk view based on a combination of those apps' enterprise-readiness. Though useful, it's only a small fraction of what you'd be able to see and doesn't include the real-time policy enforcement that you'd get with the other implementations.

- **Sanctioned app introspection via APIs:** Netskope uses secure APIs published by your sanctioned apps to control app behaviors and content residing in the apps. App introspection gives you a deep view within specific apps that you administer. It enables you to e-discover and inventory both content and users of that content. It then lets you take action on that content, including re-assigning ownership, setting sharing permissions, quarantining files, and applying encryption of data at rest.

The in-line options are

- **Agentless:** Your users' on-premises cloud network traffic is steered to the closest one of four Netskope SOC-1/SOC-2, SSAE 16 Type 2-certified datacenters around the world, which sits between your network and your cloud apps and is transparent to your users. This method provides you a "touchless" way to get on-premises cloud app network traffic from the user's PC or mobile device to the Netskope cloud for analysis. Because it sits at your network's egress point, it's limited to on-premises network traffic.
- **Thin agent or mobile profile:** Your users' remote cloud network traffic is steered to Netskope via an agent or, if a mobile device, a mobile profile. The thin agent gives you the same visibility, analytics, and enforcement as in the agentless option, but it also covers any device that's outside of the four walls of your organization.
- **Reverse proxy:** Traffic is redirected to a modified URL of your sanctioned cloud apps. The reverse proxy method gives you a "touchless" way to get cloud app visibility and control; however, it is limited to apps you administer.

Chapter 4

Creating a Cloud Security Policy

In This Chapter

- Operating in a shared-responsibility environment
- Creating data loss prevention policies
- Protecting sensitive data with encryption
- Enforcing your policies
- Educating your app users on policies
- Preventing activities that put the company at risk

When your goal is to reduce the risk of company-sensitive information getting into or being shared from your cloud apps, you need to create a cloud policy and then have an effective way to enforce the policy without compromising work getting completed.

In this chapter, you find out how to create and enforce a cloud security policy.

TIP: The better you define your cloud policy, the better everyone will understand how to leverage the cloud and reduce the risk to your organization.

Sharing Responsibility in the Cloud

With *shared responsibility,* both cloud app vendors and enterprises are responsible for a segment of cloud security:

- **Cloud app vendors selling to enterprises build apps that are inherently enterprise ready.** Apps or the vendor ecosystem should include key third-party certifications, enterprise security settings, and privacy features to meet its responsibility.
- **Enterprises ensure that their users perform safe activities within the app.** Unsafe activities include theft of confidential documents, inadvertent exposure to and disclosure of sensitive data, and compromise of authentication credentials. You maintain visibility, granular activity, and data-level control across any apps, integrated ecosystem apps, or any other cloud app your organization uses (sanctioned or unsanctioned).

As an organization consuming cloud apps, be aware and hold your vendors to their part of the shared-responsibility model, and assume responsibility for your end, which is ensuring safe usage.

Incorporating Data Loss Prevention Policies

Look to your CASB to incorporate data loss prevention (DLP) profiles into your policies. You should be able to enforce DLP policies in context, including user, app category, and so on. Some DLP profiles you may want to consider include

- **PII:** Personally identifiable information
- **PHI:** Protected health information
- **PCI:** Payment card information
- **Specific keywords:** Keywords you specify, such as for intellectual property
- **Source code**

You should also be able to create custom profiles. The content-matching profiles can be applied to any user, user group, app, app category, app instance, geo-location, device, and OS types, as shown in Figure 4-1.

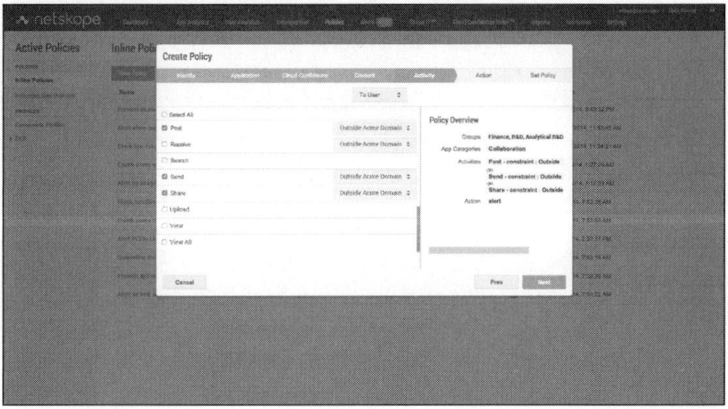

Figure 4-1: Enforce policy in context.

Be sure to pick a CASB that supports all the DLP profiles you need, whether they're predefined or custom ones that you build.

For example, if you're a healthcare company and you want to detect PHI violations, you can create a DLP profile using a predefined dictionary that contains hundreds of PHI-related classifiers (patient's name, Social Security number, medical procedures and drugs, and so on). You can also create your own classifier using pattern matching, keyword search, and regular expressions.

You can generate reports based on DLP violations. For example, you can find out which users are most often violating PCI rules, or the top apps and devices being used to violate PCI rules in the organization. You can also send these reports to other employees as attachments via email to curb policy-violating activities. Figure 4-2 shows a compliance report in the Netskope interface. You can also download it as a PDF to send to violators.

Here are some tips on creating DLP profiles in your enterprise:

- Create relevant DLP profiles for your cloud apps, including personally identifiable information, payment card information, electronic personal health information, and more.
- Base your DLP profiles on industry-standard data identifiers and rules and incorporate rich context (apps, users, time, location, and user activities) into your DLP policies.

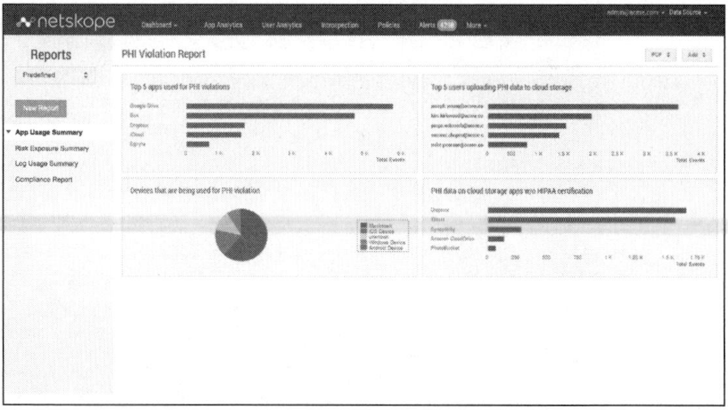

Figure 4-2: A PHI violations report.

- Discover content at rest already resident within your apps, and take action such as change ownership, quarantine content, or encrypt content.
- Set DLP policies that take effect not just in one app, but across an entire category or globally, if you need them to. Figure 4-3 shows how you can set up a DLP policy.
- Ensure that your DLP policies can be enforced in real-time before a data breach occurs.

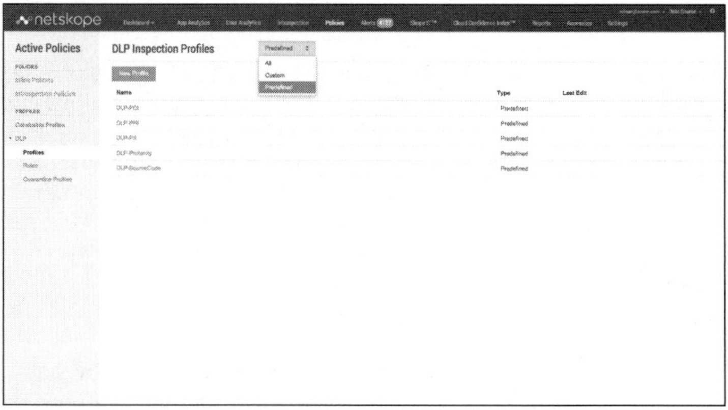

Figure 4-3: Set up your DLP profiles.

For example, if your company has an internal policy that prevents employees from including a credit card number in email, anyone who tries to do so will automatically receive a coaching message. Such a message can also be sent if he tries to send the credit card number via a cloud storage app.

As another example, if your policy only allows upload of confidential documents to Microsoft OneDrive, you can detect and block anyone who tries to upload documents using another app, and redirect the user to OneDrive.

REMEMBER

Truly preventing data loss means making users part of your compliance process. See the upcoming section "Coaching End-Users and Giving Them a Say" for more about coaching end-users on company policies. DLP ensures that your business is not interrupted or delayed.

Including Data Encryption Policies

Every policy should outline how enterprise data is encrypted:

- Where does your data reside and how is it being secured in the cloud?
- How are keys managed? In the cloud or on-premises? Are they managed according to your corporate policies? Are they held in a hardware security module? Who controls the keys?
- How will the cloud vendor handle a data breach or exposure?

These questions should be answered in your policy. Figure 4-4 shows how data travels between cloud apps and devices, between users via cloud sharing, and app-to-app.

Data at rest in an app

Data at rest refers to data that is physically stored in the cloud service provider's datacenter. Sensitive data should be protected while at rest within cloud apps. And, depending on the level of sensitivity or confidentiality, encryption standards matter. Some encryption standards you're likely to encounter include AES, RSA, DES, and each comes with a set of tradeoffs, usually along the dimensions of usability and level of protection.

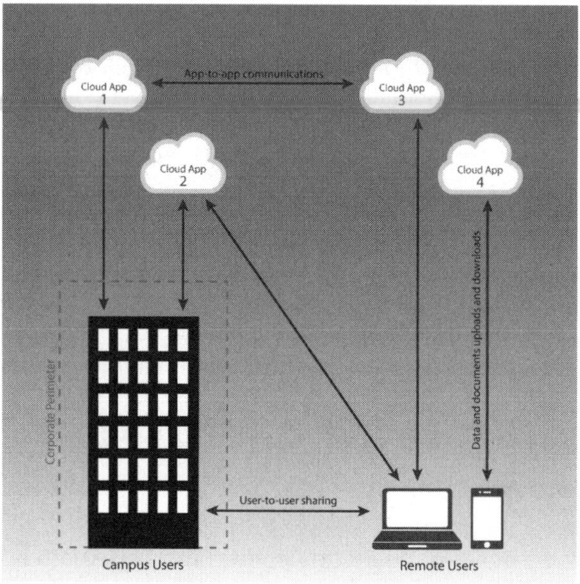

Figure 4-4: The complexity of the cloud.

TIP

For highly sensitive or confidential data, consider strong encryption such as AES-256.

When sensitive data is discovered at rest, it should be classified and inventoried. From there, you can take action such as quarantining it for legal review.

Key management is one of the most important considerations when encrypting content:

- After data is encrypted, the party that holds the keys (that can be you) has complete access to the data.
- Manage your keys with great care. If you lose the keys, your data is unusable.
- You can specify that keys be managed on-premises (versus in the cloud) and in purpose-built modules called hardware security modules (HSMs) certified

under Federal Information Processing Standard (FIPS) Publication 140-2 standard.

- Look for Key Management Interoperability Protocol (KMIP) support in a CASB, to ensure maximum compatibility with key managers in the market.

Related to encryption and key management is separation of data in the cloud. A best practice for cloud vendors dealing with business-critical data or processes is the separation of tenant data in the cloud. This is important because when customer data is co-mingled in the same cloud tenant, they run the risk of being exposed to each other. Plus, if one customer in the tenant experiences a technology failure or data corruption, all the others can be impacted as well.

Data traveling to an app

As users are uploading, sharing, editing, and downloading data, that data is at risk. Beyond encrypting data at rest, it's important that the data is secure when it's moving to and from the cloud.

Data needs to be encrypted as it moves to and from the cloud. And be sure that only authorized users have the capability to gain access to the data.

When sensitive content is discovered being uploaded into a cloud app where it's not supposed to be, the CASB should quarantine that content for review by a security, risk, or legal professional.

Data leakage

Even though in many ways cloud apps can be as secure as on-premises applications, they can also make it easy for data to be exposed or leaked. Traditional security measures tend not to cover mobile devices, where cloud apps can be accessed anywhere and anytime with any device. There's a bigger risk for an intentional or inadvertent leak. The cloud also makes it far easier than traditional computing to share data with unauthorized users and people outside the company.

For these reasons, using the cloud means that data is often out of your control. Yet you need to protect the data you can least afford to lose — your intellectual property (IP), nonpublic financials, strategic plans, customer lists, personally identifiable information belonging to customers or employees, and other sensitive data residing in your cloud apps.

A good CASB provides robust and thorough DLP capabilities covering all major file types and with support for keyword search, pattern matching, data classification, validation, proximity, and regular expression.

More than one-third (34 percent) of all data leakage policy violations (violating a DLP profile such as personally identifiable health information, payment card information, or confidential information) occur on mobile devices.

The consequences of a data breach can be huge:

- Your company could end up spending millions of dollars to remediate systems, notify customers, pay fines, and settle legal actions following a significant data breach.
- Loss of reputation following a significant data breach can have a long-lasting negative impact on company value.

Enforcing Policies

A cloud security policy is only as good as you can enforce it. Here's how:

- **Enforce activity-level and data-level policies rather than blocking apps.** You allow people to still use their favorite apps, and only block certain activities. The last section in this chapter, "Blocking Risky Activities, Not Apps," goes into greater depth.
- **Enforce policies on data whether being uploaded to, downloaded from, or residing in apps.**
    - Inspecting content as it's being uploaded to and downloaded from the cloud
    - Inspecting content that resides in your apps, regardless of when it was uploaded

TIP

Introspection is useful when you need to retrieve, encrypt, or quarantine sensitive content that resides in cloud apps. It also covers data that is uploaded by other ecosystem apps.

- **Enforce policies whether you manage the app or not.**
- **Enforce policies in real-time and in context.** This includes user, app, category, device, activity, content type, and DLP profile.
- **Coach users on policy violations**. You can direct them to the right action (like a way to sign up for a sanctioned app), or give them the opportunity to report a false positive or bypass the policy with a short justification.

Controlling cloud apps

Controlling cloud apps is a big part of enforcing a cloud policy. You can set and enforce granular policies that take effect across whatever cloud apps you specify (one app, one app instance, a category of apps, or all the cloud apps in your environment) in a few clicks.

In your CASB, you should be able to specify a variety of actions as an outcome of policy noncompliance. You can block, alert, bypass, encrypt, coach users, or begin a workflow to remediate, record, or report on an out-of-compliance event or activity.

Defining actions

There are number of actions you can take when you find company-sensitive information, as shown in Figure 4-5. You can set up a policy that

- Sends an alert when content matches your DLP profile
- Blocks cloud transactions (upload, download, and so on)
- Encrypts the content as it's being uploaded
- Quarantines the content for review by a designated IT or legal professional

For example, if you want to set sophisticated, precise policies, here's the start to a policy:

- Enable the use of collaboration apps, but prevent or closely monitor sharing of data with people outside the company.

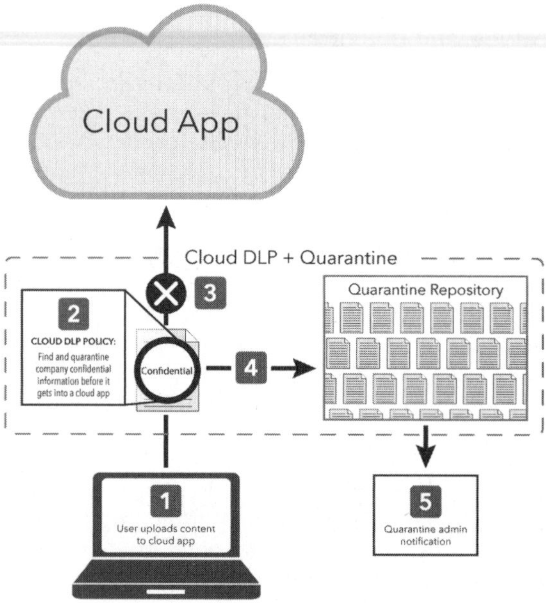

Figure 4-5: You can set up several different actions based on information.

- Disallow file uploads to cloud-storage apps that contain highly sensitive data or intellectual property that, if ever leaked, stolen, or modified, could cause serious damage to the company.
- Allow people in the HR and finance groups worldwide to access HR or finance/accounting apps, but block anyone outside the U.S. from downloading salary information.
- Allow users in sales to share any public collateral while preventing them from downloading content deemed confidential from a cloud-storage app.

- Block any user located outside your country from downloading contacts from any customer relationship management (CRM) app.
- Encrypt sensitive content in context as it's being uploaded or when it's resident within apps.
- Alert IT if any user in investor relations shares content from a finance/accounting app with someone outside the company.
- Enforce granular, specific policies on any of the visibility parameters or DLP profiles.
- Set policies once and have them enforced in real-time in any app, at the app or category level, or globally.
- Enforce policies if there is sensitive data involved, whether or not you manage the app.
- Enforce policies in real-time, before an undesired event or behavior happens.
- Allow data uploads only to apps that have a risk score of Medium or above, and block uploads to the rest.
- Coach users on policy violations to educate them about risky behaviors and to create transparency.

REMEMBER

You have to enact a cloud app policy that people can get behind. It also needs to be transparent to users and not get in the way of their experience. Otherwise, they'll simply download unsanctioned apps to get around your policy.

Coaching End-Users and Giving Them a Say

People know how their apps work. And when their apps don't work the way they expect because you've blocked the app or an activity, they get frustrated.

When you need to enforce policies, it's always a good idea to coach users. Here's why:

- You can change the way employees use apps.
- You create transparency about policy and rationale.

- You give users some control and a say in policy.
- You can change in what circumstances people use an app with a fine-grained policy.

Coaching can mean simply letting users know that you've blocked them from an activity because it's against company policy, such as the alert shown in Figure 4-6.

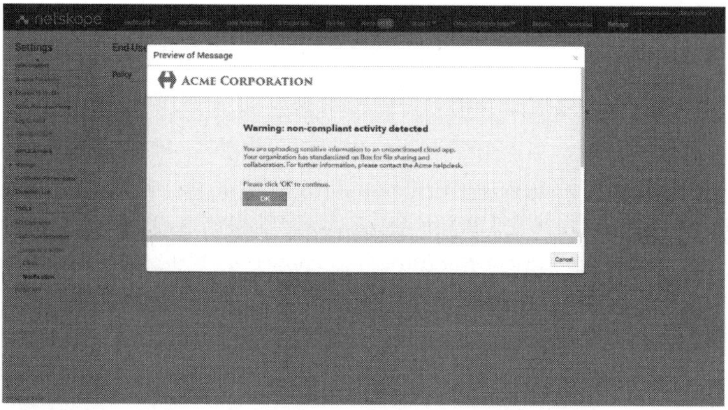

Figure 4-6: An alert telling the user he's blocked from that activity.

But even more useful is to give employees alternatives:

- **Block them from uploading content to an unsanctioned app.** You can then redirect them to a sanctioned app to upload the content.

  When an activity is blocked, a custom coaching page takes the end-user through a step-by-step process to mitigate risks.
- **Allow the activity anyway.** You can configure the system to let the user continue and enter a short justification so you can report it for compliance at a later date.
- **Let users indicate that the activity is a false positive, and let them continue.** You gather useful user feedback, making your detection and policy enforcement stronger.

When an activity is blocked, the user is routed to a coaching page giving these alternatives.

Blocking Risky Activities, Not Apps

Cloud policy enforcement doesn't need to be an all-or-nothing proposition. There's no need to block apps entirely when you can simply block risky activities from happening in apps.

Some examples of blocking activities rather than blocking apps outright include the following:

- **Downloading salary data after hours.**
- **Sharing documents outside the company during a quiet period.**
- **Uploading sensitive content to certain apps.** If a user tries to upload content to an unsanctioned storage app, you can block the upload and direct the user to a sanctioned storage app to upload the content, but still allow the user to download content from the unsanctioned app.
- **Viewing but not downloading information.** A traveling sales person may be allowed to view a customer contact (maybe to look up an address), but can't generate and download a report about all the customers from an untrusted airport Wi-Fi hotspot.

When you take a more nuanced approach — blocking risky activities rather than apps — employees will be more willing to adhere to your policy.

Chapter 5

Ten Must-Haves to Ensure Secure Usage of Cloud Apps

In This Chapter

- Discovering, segmenting, and securing your apps
- Creating policies to audit app activities, detect anomalies, and protect data
- Coaching end-users to ensure compliance

Embarking on cloud security can seem like a daunting task, even for the most experienced IT professionals. Here are ten must-haves you need to ensure that you're successful with the transition to the cloud:

- **Discover apps.** Discover the apps in your environment and assess their risk — both inherent and in the context of how they're used.
- **Segment apps.** Segment your apps by whether they're sanctioned (managed by IT) or unsanctioned (brought in by departments or by individual users).
- **Secure access.** Secure access to your sanctioned and ideally unsanctioned business apps, with single sign-on (SSO).
- **Audit activities.** Understand user activity and its context. Who's downloading from HR apps? Who's sharing content outside the company, and with whom?

- **Understand content.** Understand and classify sensitive content residing in, or traveling to or from, your cloud apps.
- **Detect anomalies.** Monitor cloud apps for anomalous activity that could signal compromised credentials, security threats, noncompliant behavior, data theft or exposure, and even malware.
- **Enforce granular policies.** Define granular policies that are enforceable in real-time, across both sanctioned and unsanctioned apps, regardless of whether users are on-network or remote, and whether in a web-based or native cloud app.
- **Protect data in context.** Have a data protection strategy. For highly sensitive content that can't be in the cloud at all, define policies that prevent it from being uploaded to any cloud app. For the next tier of content that can reside in the cloud, apply the appropriate level of security policy. This may include encrypting data before it reaches the cloud and/or limiting sharing options.
- **Ensure compliance.** Ensure regulatory compliance with continuous cloud monitoring, maintenance and review of cloud audit trails, remediation, and reporting.
- **Coach users.** Coach users both through conversations and in an automated way. Let them know when they've done something that's out of compliance (ideally in real-time, as the action is occurring), whether you block them, let them report a false positive, or let them bypass the policy with a justification.